Receiving God's Best

D1293430

Karen Heppler
210 Toucan St.
Rochester, MI 48309

Receiving God's Best

DEREK PRINCE

WHITAKER
HOUSE

Unless otherwise indicated, all Scripture quotations are taken from the Holy Bible, *New International Version*, © 1973, 1978, 1984 by the International Bible Society. Used by permission.

Scripture quotations marked (NASB) are from the *New American Standard Bible*, © 1960, 1962, 1968, 1971, 1973, 1975, 1977 by The Lockman Foundation. Used by permission.

Scripture quotations marked (NKJV) are taken from the *New King James Version*, © 1979, 1980, 1982 by Thomas Nelson, Inc. Used by permission. All rights reserved.

RECEIVING GOD'S BEST

formerly titled *If You Want God's Best*

Derek Prince
Derek Prince Ministries - International
P. O. Box 19501
Charlotte, NC 28219

ISBN: 0-88368-593-0
Printed in the United States of America
Copyright © 1985 by Derek Prince Ministries International

Whitaker House
30 Hunt Valley Circle
New Kensington, PA 15068

No part of this book may be reproduced or transmitted in any form or by any means, electronic or mechanical, including photocopying, recording, or by any information storage and retrieval system, without permission in writing from the publisher.

2 3 4 5 6 7 8 9 10 11 / 05 04 03 02 01 00

Contents

CHAPTER ONE

A Hundredfold Christian

The theme of this book is "If you want God's best...." I have stated it this way, as an incomplete sentence, on purpose. The introductory word *if* immediately confronts you with a choice. Do you want God's best, or do you not? The uncompleted second part of the sentence leaves room for me to share with you eight things you will need to do if you decide that you really *do* want God's best.

However, before I share these eight principles of success, I would like to show you how to be a hundredfold Christian.

Our personal relationship with God is never one-sided or a one-way street. There are always two sides; there are always two directions. On the one hand, there is what God makes available to us; on the other hand, there is how we respond to what God makes available. The kind of life we actually experience will be determined by the interplay of what God makes available to us and how we respond to it.

This is very clearly illustrated by the parable of the sower. (See Matthew 13:3–9, 18–23.) This parable is about a man who went out to sow seed in a field. The seed fell on four different kinds of soil. First, some seed fell beside the beaten path, and, because the ground was hard and beaten down by the feet of those who passed by, the seed never even entered the soil. As a result, the birds of the air ate the seed, and it produced nothing.

Second, some of the seed fell onto rocky ground. The seed went down a little way until its roots met rock, and it started to grow up too quickly with no depth of root. When the sun became hot, the plants withered, and this seed, too, produced nothing.

Third, some of the seed fell onto thorny ground. The thorns grew up with the plants and eventually choked them. The plants did not get enough air and nourishment, and so this seed, too, brought forth no permanent good.

I do not want to deal with the first three kinds of soil. I want to focus on what I regard as the climax of that parable, the objective to which Jesus is working, which is the good ground. I trust that you, my readers, are people whose hearts are good ground. This is what Jesus says about the good ground and the seed that fell on it:

> [23] *But the one who received the seed that fell on good soil is the man who hears the word and understands it. He produces a crop,*

yielding a hundred, sixty or thirty times what was sown.
                    (Matthew 13:23)

Notice, there are two key factors in the man who produces a crop: first, he hears the word; and second, he understands it. This is true of everybody who represents good soil. However, even though all the people who represent good soil bring forth a crop, there is a very important difference in the level of yield they produce: some produce a hundred times, some sixty times, and some only thirty times what was sown. In other words, for each seed sown, some produce a hundred seeds, some produce sixty seeds, and some produce thirty seeds.

It is interesting to observe that the hundredfold yield is more than the sum of the sixtyfold and thirtyfold yields put together. The people who really make it through to full productiveness are much more productive than the people who are only partly productive.

This principle can be found throughout the Word of God.

I want to focus on the hundredfold yield, which is representative of the people who want and achieve God's best. In another version of the same parable, found in Luke, Jesus makes this statement about the good soil:

> [15] *But the seed on good soil stands for those with a noble and good heart, who hear the word, retain it, and by persevering produce a crop.*
> *(Luke 8:15)*

In that description there are two vitally important factors, both of which are related to our theme of wanting God's best. First, there is the kind of heart, which is described as noble and good. An alternative translation for "noble" is "honest." So, the first requirement is honesty, which includes openness and sincerity. Honesty means not covering anything up or having double standards. That is the first requirement.

Second, there is a threefold response from these honest people: they hear the word; they retain it; and, by persevering, they produce a crop. Those three actions are extremely important; in fact, I want to emphasize that they are vital in acquiring God's best. Persevering, especially, is a key to acquiring God's best.

The principle unfolded in this parable confronts each of us with a personal decision. I cannot overemphasize the importance of our decisions in the walk of faith. So many people do not realize that the course of our lives depends ultimately upon the decisions we make and not on our feelings.

The decision that confronts each one of us is, How much do I intend to produce? Will I be satisfied with thirty times? Do I intend to produce sixty times? Or, am I aiming for God's best and intending to produce one hundred times? You are confronted with the necessity of making this decision. The very fact that you are reading this book automatically confronts you with a decision: Do I want God's best? Am I going to aim at a hundredfold, or be content with sixty- or thirtyfold?

What you achieve will depend on the response of your heart. I pointed out earlier that there are two sides to our relationship with God. One side is what God makes available to us; the other side is how we respond to what God makes available. The decisive factor in your life is how *you* respond.

In Luke 8:15, we saw that there are three aspects to a successful response: first, hearing God's Word; second, retaining it; and third, persevering in what you are doing.

Yes, the correct response from an honest heart will produce much fruit. And be assured that this is God's desire—to see you produce much fruit. I will discuss this in the following chapter.

CHAPTER TWO

God's Full Provision

Before moving on to the eight principles of success, I want to share two important scriptural facts related to being productive, or to bearing fruit. I believe that if you can understand these two facts, they will create in you the faith that you need to be fully productive.

God Wants Us to Be Fruitful

The first fact is this: God wants us all to be fruitful. This is a settled matter of the will of God. It is not something that is going to change. It is true right from God's creation of man. It was the very purpose for which God created man. This is stated in Genesis 1:27–28, where we read an account of God's creation of man and the purpose for which He created him.

> [27] *So God created man in his own image, in the image of God he created him; male and female he created them.*
>
> [28] *God blessed them and said to them, "Be fruitful and increase in number; fill the earth and subdue it. Rule over the fish of the sea and the birds of the air and over every living creature that moves on the ground."* (Genesis 1:27–28)

There are five things God wanted man to do:

1. Be fruitful
2. Increase
3. Fill
4. Subdue
5. Rule

These are the purposes for which man was created. God's purposes never change. Their fulfillment may be delayed by man's failure, but ultimately, God is always going to go ahead and achieve His purposes.

In the new creation, in Jesus Christ, the same purposes of God are restored once again. This is made very clear in many places in the New Testament. In particular, there is a prayer of the apostle Paul for the Christians with whom he was dealing. This beautiful prayer is recorded in Colossians 1:9–12 and has an entirely positive emphasis. Every word in this prayer is positive; there is not one negative word in the whole of this prayer.

> [9] *For this reason, since the day we heard about you, we have not stopped praying for you and asking God to fill you with the knowledge of his will through all spiritual wisdom and understanding.*

> [10] *And we pray this in order that you may live a life worthy of the Lord and may please him in every way: bearing fruit in every good work, growing in the knowledge of God,*
>
> [11] *being strengthened with all power according to his glorious might so that you may have great endurance and patience, and joyfully*
>
> [12] *giving thanks to the Father, who has qualified you to share in the inheritance of the saints in the kingdom of light.*
>
> *(Colossians 1:9–12)*

Let me point out all the positive words in this passage. First, Paul speaks about the Christians at Colosse being filled with the knowledge of God's will—not just having somewhere in them the knowledge of God's will, but being filled with it. This comes "through all spiritual wisdom and understanding" (v. 9)—not just *some*, but *all* spiritual wisdom. Then he prays that they may live a life pleasing to the Lord in every way—not just pleasing Him in some ways, but pleasing Him in every way. He prays that they may bear fruit "in every good work" (v. 10)—that is the hundredfold growing in the knowledge of God. Then, he prays that they may be "strengthened with all power according to his glorious might" (v. 11)—not *some* power, but *all* power—with the result that they may have "great endurance" (v. 11).

Perseverance, or endurance, was one of the key words in the parable of the sower. Here, Paul wants us to have great endurance and patience and joy. Finally, Paul uses the statement that God the Father has qualified us "to share in the inheritance of the saints in the kingdom of light" (v. 12). God has given us the provision that is needed to enter into our inheritance in the kingdom of light.

God's will is settled forever in the Word of God. He wants us to be fruitful;

19

He wants us to bear fruit, to succeed in every good work, and to please Him in every way. He has also qualified us, or equipped us, to do this.

We have seen already that God wants us to be fruitful in every good work. This is the will of God. There is no question about His will—the question is our response to His will.

God Has Made Full Provision

The second fact I want to emphasize is, God has made full provision for us so that we might be fruitful. We have seen from Paul's prayer that God has equipped us, or qualified us, to take our place in the "inheritance of the saints in the kingdom of light" (Colossians 1:12). This truth is brought out in many ways in the New Testament. Here is a very powerful statement that God has made full provision for this:

> [3] *His divine power has given us everything we need for life and*

godliness through our knowledge of him who called us by his own glory and goodness.

⁴ *Through these he has given us his very great and precious promises, so that through them you may participate in the divine nature and escape the corruption in the world caused by evil desires.*

(2 Peter 1:3–4)

Notice that opening phrase, "His divine power." God's total omnipotence, His unlimited power, "has given us everything we need." Let me emphasize that God *has given* us everything we need for life and godliness. This is provided in two related ways: first, "through our knowledge of him who called us" (v. 3), that is, through the knowledge of Jesus Christ; and second, through "his very great and precious promises" (v. 4). The provision comes through knowing Jesus Christ and through appropriating the promises of God's Word.

There is a saying I use in this connection that I think I can never quote too often: *The provision is in the promises*. In the promises of God's Word is contained all the provision we are ever going to need. You might say, "Well, if God has given us full provision, where is it?" The answer is that it is all in the promises of God's Word. As you appropriate those promises, you discover the provision.

There are two marvelous results of appropriating the promises. The first is that we participate in the divine nature. The very nature of God Himself comes into us, and we begin to share in His divine nature. Second, the logical negative consequence is that we escape the corruption that is in the world caused by evil desires (2 Peter 1:4). How do you feel about the possibility of becoming a partaker of God's own nature and escaping the corruption that is in this world through evil desires? Does that not appeal to you? God has made full provision for that. He has made it possible for you and me to do that. Everything we need has already been given to us.

Thus, we have two sides. The one side, your side, is *if* you want God's best; and the other side, God's side, is He *does* want it for you and has made full provision for you. So, the key decision is, Do you want God's best? That is one thing God will not do: He will not make the decision for you. You must make the decision for yourself.

In the chapters that follow, I will explain certain principles that are necessary if you want God's best. I will give you certain specific applications of these principles. The eight principles are based on three things: first, on Scripture; second, on my own personal experience, which extends well over forty years; and third, on my observation of others' experiences.

I have had the privilege of being associated with many Christians from different backgrounds, races, and countries, and I have tried to particularly observe those whom I consider to be successful, "hundredfold" people. I have tried to learn from their lives the principles of success. That is what I will be sharing with you—the principles of success, or what you will have to do if you want God's best.

CHAPTER THREE

Wanting God's Best

I n this theme, "If you want God's best," the number one requirement is to want God's best. Can you see that? If you want God's best, the first thing you have to do is make up your mind that you *do* want God's best. This is the basic, key decision. You have to want God's best, and you have to decide that you will settle for nothing less than God's best. God will not force this choice on us. It rests with us to make this decision.

I want to illustrate this principle from the story of the twin brothers,

Jacob and Esau. I will bring out of their story what I consider to be the key principle. There are some very remarkable statements made by God in Scripture about Jacob and Esau. For example, in Malachi 1:2–3 the Lord spoke to the Israelites, who are the descendants of Jacob, and said this:

> [2] *"Was not Esau Jacob's brother?"*
> [The answer is, Yes, indeed, his twin brother.]
> *"Yet I have loved Jacob,*
> [3] *but Esau I have hated."*
> *(Malachi 1:2–3)*

Notice that. They were twin brothers, but God said He loved Jacob and hated Esau. God's attitude toward the one brother was completely opposite His attitude toward the other brother. He loved one of them and hated the other. This is commented on still further by the apostle Paul in the book of Romans, where he says this concerning these twin brothers:

¹⁰ *Not only that, but Rebekah's children had one and the same father, our father Isaac.*

¹¹ *Yet, before the twins were born or had done anything good or bad—in order that God's purpose in election might stand:*

¹² *not by works but by him who calls—she* [Rebekah] *was told, "The older* [Esau] *will serve the younger* [Jacob]."

¹³ *Just as it is written: "Jacob I loved, but Esau I hated."*

(Romans 9:10–13)

Jacob and Esau were born of the same mother and the same father. Not only were they brothers, but they were twins. However, Jacob was preferred over Esau before they were ever born, even though they were twins.

This passage from Romans raises two very important questions: first, What did God see in Jacob that He approved? and second, What did God see in Esau that He disapproved? In short, why did God love Jacob but hate Esau?

Let me briefly sketch their characters for you, as unfolded in Scripture, starting with Esau. Esau was a "good guy," a "nice chap." He was strong, active, manly, a hunter. He did no one any harm. He was the favorite of his father. He was, nonetheless, no match for his shrewd twin brother, Jacob, who outdid him every time they had a confrontation.

What about Jacob? He was crafty, determined, unscrupulous. He never got the worst of a bargain. That is a quality that nobody really likes. He obtained the birthright from Esau for a bowl of soup. When his brother was hungry, he persuaded him to sell that priceless birthright for nothing more than a bowl of soup. If ever there was a bargain, that was it! He deceived his father to obtain the blessing, and he gained a fortune at the expense of Laban, who was both his uncle and his

father-in-law. By no means would anyone consider Jacob a "good guy" or a
"nice chap." By contemporary standards, most people would prefer Esau.
But God did not.

Why did God prefer Jacob? I am
going to offer you one basic reason,
which I believe is the key to it all: Jacob appreciated what God had to give,
but Esau was indifferent.

In Hebrews 12:15–17 we get a scriptural estimate of what God thinks of indifference. His views of indifference are
very different from those of most Christians. Commenting on Esau's behavior,
the writer of Hebrews says,

> [15] *See to it that no one misses the
> grace of God and that no bitter
> root grows up to cause trouble and
> defile many.*
> [16] *See that no one is sexually im-
> moral, or is godless like Esau, who
> for a single meal sold his inheri-
> tance rights as the oldest son.*

[17] *Afterward, as you know, when he wanted to inherit this blessing, he was rejected. He could bring about no change of mind, though he sought the blessing with tears.*
(Hebrews 12:15–17)

Take notice of how Esau is described. He is described as "godless," and he is put on the same level with the sexually immoral. He is also described as godless because for a single meal, a bowl of soup, he sold his inheritance rights. As we are told in Genesis 25:34, "Esau *despised* his birthright" (italics added). You must understand that by God's standards, indifference concerning what God has to offer is "godless," and God hates it.

Let us look at the opposite side, Jacob's attitude toward what God had to offer. I will take just one key incident. Jacob was on his way back to his own land when he met a man at night, who was also an angel or a messenger from God. As you will remember, he wrestled

with this man all night. This is typical
of Jacob because he was a wrestler; he
was always fighting to be on top.

> [24] *So Jacob was left alone, and a
> man wrestled with him till day-
> break.*
> [25] *When the man saw that he could
> not overpower him, he touched the
> socket of Jacob's hip so that his
> hip was wrenched as he wrestled
> with the man.*
> [26] *Then the man said, "Let me go,
> for it is daybreak." But Jacob re-
> plied, "I will not let you go unless
> you bless me."*
> [27] *The man asked him, "What is
> your name?" "Jacob," he an-
> swered.*
> [28] *Then the man said, "Your name
> will no longer be Jacob, but Israel,
> because you have struggled with
> God and with men and have over-
> come."* (Genesis 32:24–28)

The meaning of "Israel," as here
interpreted, is "struggling with God."

How typical! Jacob was a struggler, a wrestler. However, he had one key principle: he wanted God's best. He said to this angel, "I will not let you go unless you bless me" (v. 26). I believe that was the key to God's favor toward Jacob. God did not condone the flaws in Jacob's character; God never does condone character flaws. But, because Jacob would not settle for less than God's best, God was gradually able to deal with him and to make out of him the kind of man He wanted him to be. The condition, and the starting point, was that Jacob would not settle for anything less than God's best.

I want to ask you, Will you make the same decision, that you will not settle for anything less than God's best?

CHAPTER FOUR

Jesus, Our Focus

There is a second way to complete the sentence, "If you want God's best...." It is *focus on Jesus*. We are told in the twelfth chapter of Hebrews,

> [1] *Therefore, since we are surrounded by such a great cloud of witnesses, let us throw off everything that hinders and the sin that so easily entangles, and let us run with perseverance the race marked out for us.*
> [2] *Let us fix our eyes on Jesus, the author and perfecter of our faith,*

who for the joy set before him en-
dured the cross, scorning its
shame, and sat down at the right
hand of the throne of God.
                    (Hebrews 12:1–2)

There are a number of logical steps
in what the writer says. First, he points
out that we are surrounded by a great
cloud of witnesses. He is referring to
the previous chapter of Hebrews (chapter 11), where he wrote about the great
saints of the Old Testament who suc-
ceeded—men who found God's best.
The writer says we have a cloud of witnesses around us, people who have
proved in their lives and experiences
that it really is possible to find God's
best. That is the starting point.

Second, he says that if we want to
find God's best, doing so will consist in
running a race. In order to run the race
successfully, we must throw off everything that hinders. A runner does not
carry a single ounce of unnecessary
weight on his person or in his clothing.

In our case, it is sin that so easily entangles us, and we must be sure there is nothing to trip us up.

Third, we must run with perseverance. I pointed out earlier, in connection with the good soil in the parable of the sower, that the three conditions were hearing the Word, retaining the Word, and bringing forth fruit with perseverance.

Having laid those foundations for success, the writer of Hebrews now comes to what I consider to be the critical point: "Let us fix our eyes on Jesus, the author and perfecter of our faith" (Hebrews 12:2). This is a key to success: focus on Jesus; keep your eyes on Him. The writer points out that Jesus is both the author and perfecter of our faith.

I will use two simpler words: He is the beginner and completer of our faith. We probably all realize that Jesus is the beginner, but sometimes we forget the fact that Jesus is also the completer. If we want our faith to be completed, we have to keep on focusing on Jesus. It is not enough to begin by focusing on Jesus and then get distracted and look somewhere else. If we do that, our faith will never be completed.

In this connection, I want to point out to you four simple facts, each of which is a reason why we should continue to focus on Jesus.

Jesus, Our Lord

Jesus is our Lord. We can only enter into salvation through confessing Jesus as our Lord. If He is our Lord, then our supreme purpose is to please Him. That is what it means when we say that He is our Lord. We need to continually keep our eyes on Jesus, to make sure that everything we are doing pleases Him. If at any time, as we look at Him, we get an indication that what we are considering would not please Him, that is a sufficient reason for not doing it. But we cannot receive such an indication unless we keep our eyes fixed on Jesus.

Jesus, Our Standard

Jesus is the only standard of righteousness. This is brought out by a statement that Paul made to the men of Athens:

> [31] "[God] *has appointed a day on which He will judge the world in righteousness by the Man whom He has ordained. He has given assurance of this to all by raising Him from the dead."*
>
> *(Acts 17:31 NKJV)*

The one who is going to be God's Judge of the world is the Man whom He raised from the dead, Jesus Christ. God is going to judge the world in righteousness by that Man.

That tells us two things: Jesus is the Judge, and He is also our standard of righteousness. We are going to be judged by the standard of Jesus. It is important to see that God has only one standard of righteousness. If we want to know what is righteous in the eyes of God, the ultimate place we must look is always Jesus. We may look at Christians, but they do things that Jesus would not have done. We cannot accept them as our standard of righteousness, because they are not God's standard. To find out God's standard of righteousness, we must keep our eyes focused on Jesus.

Jesus, Our Example

Jesus is our pattern or our example, as we see in the book of First Peter:

> [21] *To this you were called, because Christ suffered for you, leaving you an example, that you should follow in his steps.* (1 Peter 2:21)

Jesus is our example because He has gone before us. To follow in the right path, we must see where He planted His steps and plant our footsteps in the same places. All of that is involved in this one important requirement: that we focus on Jesus by keeping our eyes fixed on Him.

Jesus, the Heart of the Gospel

I want to give you one more reason why it is necessary to focus on Jesus. It is a very simple reason, a very practical reason, but a very important one. The whole Gospel centers on what Jesus has done for us. This is stated clearly by Paul in First Corinthians. Notice, there are orders of importance in the things of God, but the things that Paul writes of here are "of first importance." He makes three simple statements, each of which relates to Jesus:

> [3] *For what I received I passed on to you as of first importance: that Christ died for our sins according to the Scriptures,*

⁴ that he was buried, that he was raised on the third day according to the Scriptures.

(1 Corinthians 15:3–4)

That is the Gospel. Those are the facts of first importance. Everything else in the Gospel is of secondary importance compared with those three facts, all of which center on Jesus: He died, He was buried, and He rose again the third day. We can never afford to let anything else become more important than those three facts about Jesus. We must be careful never to be enticed away from those basic truths, which are centered on Jesus.

Paul warns Timothy of this in his second epistle to Timothy, written from prison very near the end of his life:

⁸ Remember Jesus Christ, raised from the dead, descended from David. This is my gospel,

> [9] *for which I am suffering even to the point of being chained like a criminal. But God's word is not chained.* *(2 Timothy 2:8–9)*

Take note of those key words: "Remember Jesus Christ, raised from the dead....This is my gospel." How simple! It is just like what he said in 1 Corinthians 15—the whole gospel message centers on Jesus: His death, His burial, and His victorious resurrection.

Paul also tells Timothy to never get distracted from these central points, but to keep his eyes focused on Jesus.

There is a great danger for Christians to become too sophisticated or too spiritual. Many Christians lose out by becoming too spiritual. People sometimes say to me after I preach, "Brother Prince, that was a deep message." And I find myself wondering, "Did I do something wrong?" In a certain sense, I do not want to go too deep.

41

I never want to go so deep that people lose sight of Jesus and the central facts of the Gospel: His death, His burial, and His resurrection.

Let me exhort you with what Paul said to Timothy: "Remember Jesus Christ, raised from the dead" (2 Timothy 2:8). One very important and practical way to remember Jesus is through the taking of Communion, or the Lord's Supper. Jesus said, "This do, as often as you [do] it, in remembrance of Me" (1 Corinthians 11:25 NKJV). It is a very simple, scriptural, practical way to remember Jesus and to keep your eyes focused on Him. Remember, He said, "As *often* as you do it," not as seldom as you do it. Jesus wants us to keep our eyes continually focused on Him.

CHAPTER FIVE

Meditating on God's Word

A third thing that is most important for you to do if you want God's best is to meditate on God's Word. Fill your mind with the Word of God. Take a look at the example of Joshua and the instructions the Lord gave him as he was about to lead Israel into their inheritance.

[8] *This Book of the Law shall not depart from your mouth, but you shall meditate in it day and night, that you may observe to do according to all that is written in it. For then you will make your*

*way prosperous, and then you will
have good success.*

(Joshua 1:8 NKJV)

That last part, "you will make your
way prosperous, and then you will have
good success," is equivalent to saying,
"you will find God's best." What are
the conditions? There are three of
them, and they all relate to God's
Word:

1. The Word is "not [to] depart
   from your mouth."
2. You are to "meditate in it day
   and night"—that means continually.
3. You are to "observe to do according to all that is written in
   it."

I have sometimes summed it up in
three simple phrases. If you want
God's best, if you want to make your
way prosperous and have good success,
these are the three things you must do:

think God's Word, *speak* God's Word, and *act* God's Word. I put thinking first because if you do not think, you will never fully speak. If you do not think and speak, you will never fully act. The result of doing all three is success—God's best.

You might say, "That was Joshua. How do I know that will work for me?" The first Psalm has a similar promise with a similar instruction, and it is for anybody who meets the conditions. It is all-inclusive. It does not matter who the person is; all that matters is that the person meets the conditions.

> [1] *Blessed is the man who does not walk in the counsel of the wicked or stand in the way of sinners or sit in the seat of mockers.*
>
> [2] *But his delight is in the law of the LORD, and on his law he meditates day and night.*
>
> [3] *He is like a tree planted by streams of water, which yields its fruit in season and whose leaf does*

not wither. Whatever he does pros-
pers. (Psalm 1:1–3)

Take note of the closing sentence:
"Whatever he does prospers." That is
finding God's best; that is true success.
This can be true of any man who meets
the conditions. The conditions are five-
fold. The first three are negative; in
other words, they are things you must
not do:

1. You must not walk in the counsel of the wicked.
2. You must not stand in the way
   of sinners.
3. You must not sit in the seat of
   mockers.

The key issue is where you get your
counsel. If you get your counsel from
the wrong source, then your whole life
will go wrong. The three negative conditions are then followed by two positive conditions:

1. Your delight must be in the law of the Lord.
2. On His law, you must meditate day and night.

Notice that both of the positive conditions center on the law of the Lord, or the Word of God. First, you have to delight yourself in His law. Second, you have to meditate on it day and night. Notice again that right meditation is the key to success—meditating on God's Word day and night.

That does not mean just spending ten minutes a day reading your Bible, but it means to so fill your mind with the Bible that it occupies your thoughts all the day long. Then you will always be feeding on that which is positive, faith-inspiring, and upbuilding. Right thoughts are important, for what you think will decide how you live.

I have sometimes said that human personality is like an iceberg: seven-eighths is below the surface. Very little of the iceberg actually shows above the surface in comparison with what is below the surface. It is also true with human personality.

What a person is thinking about is going to determine the course of his or her life. If you meditate on the right things and live the right kind of life, then you will get the results that God has promised: success and prosperity— God's best.

Take a look at a passage, from the prophet Isaiah, that reiterates that the way we think affects our experience. God is speaking in this passage:

> [8] *"For my thoughts are not your thoughts, neither are your ways my ways," declares the LORD.*
>
> [9] *"As the heavens are higher than the earth, so are my ways higher than your ways and my thoughts than your thoughts.*
>
> [10] *"As the rain and the snow come down from heaven, and do not return to it without watering the*

> *earth and making it bud and
> flourish, so that it yields seed for
> the sower and bread for the eater,*
>
> [11] *"so is my word that goes out
> from my mouth."* (Isaiah 55:8–11)

Notice, God begins with thoughts, and He says that, by nature, our thoughts are not His thoughts. How, then, can we begin to think God's thoughts? God gives the answer in the words that follow. God's ways and God's thoughts are on the heavenly plane, and our ways and our thoughts are on the earthly plane, far below God's. But God's Word brings His ways and His thoughts down from heaven into our lives and hearts, producing the results we need.

God goes on to say in the same passage, concerning His Word:

> [11] *"It will not return to me empty,
> but will accomplish what I desire
> and achieve the purpose for which
> I sent it.*

> [12] *"You will go out in joy and be led forth in peace; the mountains and hills will burst into song before you, and all the trees of the field will clap their hands.*
>
> [13] *"Instead of the thornbush will grow the pine tree, and instead of briers the myrtle will grow."*
>
> *(Isaiah 55:11–13)*

This is the result of God's Word coming down from heaven, entering our hearts, occupying our minds, and replacing our ways and our thoughts with God's ways and God's thoughts. God's Word brings His ways and thoughts down to our hearts and lives. As our minds are filled with the Word of God, we begin to think the thoughts of God. Our whole thought life is completely changed.

The results are stated here in beautiful language: peace (you will be led forth with peace), joy (you will go out with joy), praise (even the things of nature will praise—"the trees of the

field will clap their hands"), and fruit-
fulness (in place of the thornbush and
the brier, the myrtle and the pine will
grow). That is what happens in our
lives when God's Word comes in and
we receive it and begin to meditate on
it. Our own ways and our own thoughts
are like the thorns and the briers; they
are unproductive and unhelpful. But
when they are replaced by God's Word,
then instead of the thorn and the brier,
we bring forth the pine and the myrtle.

I want to suggest that you should
view the substitution of God's ways and
God's thoughts for your own ways and
thoughts as being the key to success.
You should also cultivate the practice of
meditating on God's Word day and
night. Meditating on God's Word is
learning to think God's thoughts by receiving His Word into our hearts and
minds.

CHAPTER SIX

Friendship with the Holy Spirit

The fourth thing you must do if you want God's best, is to make friends with the Holy Spirit. I deliberately use a phrase that suggests the personality of the Holy Spirit. For many Christians, the Holy Spirit is a kind of theological abstraction. They accept that God the Father is a person, they accept that Jesus Christ is a person, but they have no concept that the Holy Spirit is a person. Yet, scripturally and theologically, this is a fact. The Holy Spirit is a person just as much as the Father and the Son.

He is also compared to a dove. One of the important features of a dove is that it is a timid creature, and if you do not respond in the right way to the presence of a dove, it will just fly off. I think that is true of the Holy Spirit. In a certain sense, He is timid. If we do not respond to Him the right way, He just withdraws.

In the following passage of Scripture, Jesus speaks to His disciples about the Holy Spirit as a person and what the Holy Spirit will do in our lives:

> *12 I have much more to say to you, more than you can now bear.*
>
> *13 But when he, the Spirit of truth, comes, he will guide you into all truth. He will not speak on his own; he will speak only what he hears, and he will tell you what is yet to come.*
>
> *14 He will bring glory to me by taking from what is mine and making it known to you.*

> ¹⁵ *All that belongs to the Father is*
> *mine. That is why I said the Spirit*
> *will take from what is mine and*
> *make it known to you.*
> *(John 16:12–15)*

First, Jesus does everything that
language permits to emphasize the
personality of the Holy Spirit by saying, "But when he, the Spirit of truth,
comes." In the Greek language, in
which these words were originally
given to us, there are three genders:
masculine, feminine, and neuter. Neuter is the "it" gender. In Greek, the
word for "spirit," *pneuma*, is neuter. In
other words, the normal pronoun to
use with "spirit" would be "it." But Jesus breaks the law of grammar and
says not "when *it*," but "when *he*, the
Spirit of truth, comes" (italics added).
In other words, He goes out of His way
to emphasize that we are dealing with
a person.

Jesus then speaks about various
things the Holy Spirit will do. He will

report on what He hears from heaven by bringing us the latest news from heaven; He will show us what is yet to come by unfolding the future to us.

Then Jesus says, "He will bring glory to me by taking from what is mine and making it known to you. All that belongs to the Father is mine" (John 16:14–15). That is extremely important. Everything the Father has belongs to the Son, and everything the Son has, the Spirit administers. If you put that together, the Holy Spirit is the administrator of the total wealth of the Godhead. All that the Father has and all that the Son has, they have in common. But it is the Holy Spirit who takes from the wealth of the Father and the Son and makes it available to us. Thus, you can be a child of God legally and doctrinally, and yet live a very poor and inadequate kind of life unless you relate rightly to the Holy Spirit, because the Holy Spirit is the administrator of the total wealth of the Godhead.

Again, in the book of John, Jesus says to His disciples:

> [15] *"If you love me, you will obey what I command.*
>
> [16] *"And I will ask the Father, and he will give you another Counselor to be with you forever—*
>
> [17] *"the Spirit of truth. The world cannot accept him, because it neither sees him nor knows him. But you know him, for he lives with you and will be in you.*
>
> [18] *"I will not leave you as orphans; I will come to you."*
>
> *(John 14:15–18)*

Notice two vitally important facts: first, Jesus comes to us in the Holy Spirit; second, unless we relate rightly to the Holy Spirit, we are like orphans even though we are truly sons of God. You see, it is the Holy Spirit alone who enables us to live as true sons of God. This is brought out very clearly by Paul in Romans 8:14 (NKJV): "For as many as are led by the Spirit of God [and that is a continuing present tense—as many as are being *continually led* by the Spirit of God], these are sons of God."

The word that is used for "sons" here implies maturity—not merely babies or infants, but grown sons of God. We are babies when we become born again by the Holy Spirit. But, in order to become mature sons of God, we need a further, ongoing relationship with the Holy Spirit. We must be continually led by the Holy Spirit; thus Paul says very definitively, "As many as are [being continually] led by the Spirit of God, these are [mature] sons of God." Thus, to become a child of God, you have to be born again of the Holy Spirit; but, to become a mature son of God, you must have an ongoing relationship by being daily and continually led by the Holy Spirit.

I observe in the church today that there are many who are truly born of God but who are not regularly led by

God. They know the new birth, but they do not know that continuing relationship with the Holy Spirit that alone can enable them to live as mature sons of God. So, if you want God's best, you must cultivate an ongoing relationship with the Holy Spirit as a person. He is your personal guide, the administrator of the riches of the kingdom of God, who alone can impart all these things to you in experience.

There is one further important fact in our relationship with the Holy Spirit. We must be respectful and sensitive toward the Holy Spirit. Paul brings this out clearly in his letter to the Ephesians:

> [30] *And do not grieve the Holy Spirit of God, with whom you were sealed for the day of redemption.*
>
> [31] *Get rid of all bitterness, rage and anger, brawling and slander, along with every form of malice.*
> *(Ephesians 4:30–31)*

Remember that we said at the beginning that the Holy Spirit is compared to a dove, a timid bird that is easily scared away. So, when Paul says, "Do not grieve the Holy Spirit," he means, "Don't scare that dove away." He then mentions the things that scare the dove: bitterness, rage, anger, brawling, slander, along with every form of malice. We must be very sensitive, not saying or doing anything that would frighten away that beautiful, sensitive dove, because He is the only one who can bring us into our inheritance and enable us to live daily as mature sons of God.

CHAPTER SEVEN

Hearing and Obeying

We now come to a fifth way to complete the sentence, "If you want God's best...." You must learn to *hear and obey God's voice*.

This is not something that comes to us naturally. In a certain sense, the old Adamic nature is born deaf to the voice of God. It is not natural for the old carnal nature to hear God's voice. It is something that must be learned and cultivated with care. The world today is full of innumerable voices that blast us, that crowd in upon us, that demand our attention. Yet, in the midst of it all, there is that still, small voice of God, which has endless wisdom and authority, and which is the key to our well-being.

I want to suggest to you that there is tremendous motivation revealed in Scripture for cultivating the ability to hear the voice of God. The success of our relationship with God and our walk with Him depends on hearing His voice.

I will give a few specific examples. The first is in the matter of receiving healing and health from God. Without question, the Scripture makes it clear that the key to healing and health is the ability to hear God's voice. This is brought out clearly in Exodus 15:26, in which Moses is speaking to the children of Israel:

26 If you diligently heed the voice of the LORD your God and do what is right in His sight, give ear to His commandments and keep all His

statutes, I will put none of the dis-
eases on you which I have brought
on the Egyptians. For I am the
LORD who heals you.
                    (Exodus 15:26 NKJV)

The Hebrew text says, "If hearing, you hear the voice of the Lord your God." That is a Hebraism, a very emphatic form of the language. It means to listen with the most tremendous care to the voice of the Lord your God. Then God offers to be your personal physician. But the basic condition is to diligently listen to the voice of the Lord.

In Deuteronomy 28, Moses reveals that the key to all God's blessings is hearing and obeying His voice:

[1]*Now it shall come to pass, if you diligently obey the voice of the LORD your God, to observe carefully all His commandments which I command you today, that the LORD your God will set you high above all nations of the earth.*

> ² *And all these blessings shall*
> *come upon you and overtake you,*
> *because you obey the voice of the*
> *LORD your God.*
>> *(Deuteronomy 28:1–2 NKJV)*

Notice, twice Moses says that the key condition is hearing and obeying the voice of God. He says if you do that, "all these blessings shall come upon you and overtake you." You do not need to pursue the blessings; they will pursue you if you cultivate hearing the voice of God. On the other hand, a little farther on, in verse 15, he warns that if we fail to hear the voice of the Lord our God, it will be the exact opposite: instead of blessings will be curses.

> ¹⁵ *But it shall come to pass, if you*
> *do not obey the voice of the LORD*
> *your God, to observe carefully all*
> *His commandments and His stat-*
> *utes which I command you today,*
> *that all these curses will come*
> *upon you and overtake you.*
>> *(Deuteronomy 28:15 NKJV)*

So, failure to hear and obey the voice of the Lord brings upon us all the curses; hearing and obeying brings all the blessings. That is the watershed between blessing and cursing. We can either hear and obey the voice of the Lord, or we can fail to hear and obey the voice of the Lord.

In Jeremiah 7, the Lord lays down the key condition for being His people. He says to Israel:

> [22] *For I did not speak to your fathers, or command them in the day that I brought them out of the land of Egypt, concerning burnt offerings or sacrifices.*
> [23] *But this is what I commanded them, saying, "Obey My voice, and I will be your God, and you shall be My people."*
> *(Jeremiah 7:22–23 NKJV)*

God is saying here that the ordinances of the law relating to the temple, the priesthood, and the sacrifices are secondary. The first thing that He required of His people when He brought them out of Egypt was not sacrifice, offering, or a lot of legal requirements. Rather, He required them to hear and obey His voice. By implication, He is saying that the sacrifices are good if they proceed out of hearing His voice, but if the people were to merely offer sacrifices without hearing His voice, it would not qualify them to be His people. They would be His people only if they would hear and obey His voice.

That is the most concise statement in Scripture about what it is to be God's people: "Obey My voice, and I will be your God, and you shall be My people" (Jeremiah 7:23 NKJV).

This does not change in the New Testament, where the condition for belonging to Jesus Christ is just the same. Jesus states it very simply in John 10:27 (NKJV): "My sheep hear My voice, and I know them, and they follow Me."

Who are "My sheep"? They are the people of Jesus. They are not necessarily Catholics, Protestants, Baptists, Methodists, or any other particular denomination. The people who belong to Jesus are the people who hear His voice and follow Him. If you do not hear His voice, you cannot follow Him. That is always the mark of God's true people: they hear His voice.

Cultivate Prompt Obedience

I want to give you two important warnings in connection with this theme of hearing God's voice. First, cultivate prompt obedience—and I want to emphasize *prompt*. Abraham is set forth in the Bible as an example for all who believe, and one of the ways in which he is an example is that whenever he heard God's voice, he obeyed Him promptly, without delay. Here is an example:

> [2] *Then He said, "Take now your son, your only son Isaac, whom*

67

you love, and go to the land of Mo-
riah, and offer him there as a
burnt offering on one of the moun-
tains of which I shall tell you."

³ *So Abraham rose early in the*
morning and saddled his donkey,
and took two of his young men
with him, and Isaac his son.

(Genesis 22:2–3 NKJV)

Notice, Abraham rose early in the
morning the next day. As soon as it
was possible, he set out to obey what
he had heard God say to him. I can tell
you from experience and from observation that the longer you delay to obey
God, the harder it becomes. The only
easy way to obey God is to obey Him
promptly, the first time He speaks.

Let us look at a negative example.
Somebody who delayed in obeying God
was Lot's wife. She was willing to come
out of Sodom, but she came so slowly
she never made it. She looked back and
was turned into a pillar of salt. One of
the shortest verses in the teaching of

Jesus is Luke 17:32: "Remember Lot's wife!" In other words, do not delay to obey, or it may be too late.

Be Prepared to Seem Foolish

The second warning I want to give you is, Be prepared to seem foolish in the eyes of other people. In 1 Corinthians 1:25 (NKJV) Paul says, "The foolishness of God is wiser than men, and the weakness of God is stronger than men." If you believe that what people think is wise, you may miss God. In his same letter to the Corinthians, Paul is very emphatic:

> [18] *Let no one deceive himself. If anyone among you seems to be wise in this age, let him become a fool that he may become wise.*
> *(1 Corinthians 3:18 NKJV)*

To become truly wise, you have to start by becoming a fool. Many people stumble over that, but there are many examples in the Bible. Noah built a ship on dry land when no one had ever seen rain. That was foolish, but it was the wisdom of God. Naaman, the captain of Syria, went down into the Jordan River and exposed his leprous flesh by dipping himself seven times. How foolish! But he was healed. Then, in John 9, there was the man who had been born blind. Jesus placed clay on his eyes and then told him to go and wash in the pool of Siloam. How foolish he must have looked, groping his way to the pool of Siloam with clay on his eyes! But he was healed.

There was a situation in my own life years ago when I was preaching in East Africa. I held a seven-day series of services, and at the end of each message I said, "If anyone wants me to pray for his healing, stand up and I'll pray for you." There was a blind woman led to the meeting by a boy; every day for six days she stood up, I prayed, and nothing happened. I became embarrassed for her. The seventh day she was there again. I said, "If you want me to pray for your healing, stand up!" She stood. I closed my eyes and prayed, but I could not help wondering, "What's going to happen to that poor woman?" When I opened my eyes, there she was, walking forward without the boy to show that her eyes had been healed! You see, she had to be willing to become a fool first.

CHAPTER EIGHT

Two
Hearing
Tests

A sixth way to complete the sentence, "If you want God's best..." is *be careful how and what you hear*. Obviously, this relates closely to the previous chapter's theme of hearing and obeying God's voice. We are going on with this theme of hearing.

I have already pointed out that all through the Bible, from the Old Testament into the New, the basic requirement for belonging to God's people is hearing and obeying His voice. In the Old Testament, God said to Israel,

"Obey My voice, and I will be your God, and you shall be My people" (Jeremiah 7:23 NKJV). In the New Testament, Jesus said, "My sheep hear My voice, and I know them, and they follow Me" (John 10:27 NKJV). That requirement never changes in any dispensation or any age.

We will now consider more of what is involved in hearing God's voice. Jesus said two things at different times in the Gospels. He said, "Take heed what you hear," and later on He said, "Take heed how you hear." Let us examine both of these statements and see what they have to say to us.

What You Hear

The first one, "what you hear," is in Mark 4:23–25, where Jesus begins, "If anyone has ears to hear, let him hear." I understand that to mean, "If anyone has ears to hear God's voice, let him hear." I pointed out that we are not born naturally with the ability to hear God's voice. It is something that must be imparted to us by the Holy Spirit. It is something that must be cultivated.

Jesus goes on to say,

> ²⁴ *Take heed what you hear. With the same measure you use, it will be measured to you; and to you who hear, more will be given.*
> ²⁵ *For whoever has, to him more will be given; but whoever does not have, even what he has will be taken away from him.*
> *(Mark 4:24–25 NKJV)*

Jesus unfolds three principles here. First, the basic requirement is having the ability to hear, that is, to hear God's voice. "If anyone has ears to hear, let him hear."

Second, by right hearing (or by listening to the right thing), we increase our spiritual resources. "To you who hear," Jesus says, "more will be given." The same measure that you use will be measured back to you. The more you give of yourself to hearing God's voice, the more God will give Himself back to you. In other words, *we* settle the measure with which God will give Himself to us. The measure with which we hear is the measure with which God will impart Himself to us.

The third principle is that by wrong hearing (or failure to hear), we decrease our spiritual resources and finally become spiritually bankrupt. Jesus says, "Whoever has, to him more will be given; but whoever does not have, even what he has will be taken away from him" (Mark 4:25 NKJV). In my experience, I have encountered Christians who seem to be totally bankrupt, yet in past years they were abounding in the blessing of the Lord. What bankrupted them? They had lost the ability to hear (had ceased to cultivate that ability) and had begun to listen to the wrong things.

They had cut God off and opened themselves up to evil, negative sources, which had bankrupted them spiritually.

How You Hear

Jesus also tells us to be careful how we hear.

> [18] *Therefore take heed how you hear. For whoever has, to him more will be given; and whoever does not have, even what he seems to have will be taken from him.*
> *(Luke 8:18 NKJV)*

Again, we find the same solemn warning. The way in which we open up to hear God will determine the way in which God imparts Himself to us. But, if we shut God out by wrong hearing, then we become bankrupt. Jesus repeats the same principle—the principle of increase or decrease according to what we hear and how we hear.

I want to mention another principle about how to hear: we must learn what to accept and what to reject. There is a very pertinent statement in Job 12:11: "Does not the ear test words as the tongue tastes food?"

The ear fulfills the same function in regard to words as the mouth does in regard to what we eat. We all know that if we put something into our mouth that is bitter or unpleasant, we do not swallow it; we spit it out. What that statement in Job is saying is that our ears need to do the same to what we hear. If we hear something that is bitter, negative, or destructive to our faith, then we should not accept it; we should reject it.

Just as the tongue tastes food, the ear tests words. I have often said to people, "When you listen to a preacher (or whoever is talking), do what you do when you eat fish: swallow the meat and spit out the bones. If you swallow the bones, you are going to be sorry for it." That is my simple application of what Jesus meant when He said, "Take heed how you hear." Let the right thing in, but keep the wrong thing out. If you let the wrong thing in, you will regret it.

Faith Comes

Another principle that relates to hearing is stated in Romans 10:17 (NKJV): "So then faith comes by hearing, and hearing by the word of God."

That is a tremendously important truth: "faith comes." You do not need to be without faith. I remember a time when I was without faith. I was sick in a hospital for one year, and doctors could not heal me. I was hopeless. But one day the Holy Spirit quickened that statement to me, "Faith comes." If you do not have faith, you can get it. How do you get it? By hearing. Hearing what? The Word of God. I began to hear God's Word, and through it faith came, until eventually I was released from the hospital. I was healed, not by medical means, but by the supernatural power of God, because I received faith through hearing the Word of God.

The important thing that I want to emphasize is this: not only does faith come by hearing, but unbelief comes by hearing, too. Paul says this in 2 Timothy 2:16–18, where he is advising Timothy about how to lead a successful Christian life.

> [16] *Avoid godless chatter, because those who indulge in it will become more and more ungodly.*
>
> [17] *Their teaching will spread like gangrene [or cancer; the word in the original text means both]. Among them are Hymenaeus and Philetus,*
>
> [18] *who have wandered away from the truth. They say that the resurrection has already taken place, and they destroy the faith of some.*
>
> *(2 Timothy 2:16–18)*

Paul is saying that if you want to keep your faith, you should not listen to godless chatter or the likes of Hymenaeus and Philetus, who were spreading false teaching. If you go on hearing it, it will enter into your heart and mind and will eat away your faith just like a cancer eats away sound flesh. Cultivate, instead, the practice of right hearing, in both what you hear and how you hear. Faith comes by hearing the Word of God.

As a logical safeguard, choose your friends and associates with care, because they will be the people to whom you will listen the most. You will want to listen to people who have something good to say, not something that destroys your faith.

[14] *Do not be yoked together with unbelievers. For what do righteousness and wickedness have in common? Or what fellowship can light have with darkness?*

(2 Corinthians 6:14)

> ¹¹ *Have nothing to do with the fruitless deeds of darkness, but rather expose them.*
> ¹² *For it is shameful even to mention what the disobedient do in secret.* (Ephesians 5:11–12)

Do not associate with people whose speech and conduct are evil. It will poison you spiritually. On the positive side, Paul says this to Timothy:

> ²² *Flee the evil desires of youth, and pursue righteousness, faith, love and peace, along with those who call on the Lord out of a pure heart.* (2 Timothy 2:22)

In other words, if you are going to pursue the good things, you must pursue them in the right company, with people who call on the Lord out of a pure heart.

CHAPTER NINE

Proper Priorities

The seventh way to complete the sentence, "If you want God's best...," is *be more concerned with the eternal than with the temporal.*

There is a passage of Scripture in which the eternal and the temporal are set side by side and compared.

> [17] *For our light affliction, which is but for a moment, is working for us a far more exceeding and eternal weight of glory,*
> [18] *while we do not look at the things which are seen, but at the things which are not seen. For the*

> *things which are seen are tempo-*
> *rary, but the things which are not*
> *seen are eternal.*
>   *(2 Corinthians 4:17–18 NKJV)*

Paul says there are two categories of things: the eternal and the temporary. The temporary things are the things we can see, the things of this world that we contact with our senses. But the eternal things are unseen. They belong to the invisible, eternal world. He brings out a tremendously important principle: our light affliction works for us an eternal weight of glory while we are looking, not at the things that are seen, but at the things that are not seen.

Most of us are going to go through affliction; we must face that fact. Sooner or later in life, we are going to face trouble, hardship, or difficulty, which will do for us something of eternal value on one basic condition: *that we continue looking at the things that are not seen*. But, if we take our eyes off the eternal things and begin to look only at the temporary things, at the things of this world that we contact with our natural senses, then our affliction is no longer working for us that eternal glory that it is God's purpose for us to have.

When we come into trouble or affliction, it is very important that we learn to respond in the right way. We must not be distracted from the eternal by problems and troubles, but we must keep our eyes steadfastly fixed on the eternal and unseen.

Paul deliberately expresses a paradox here when he talks about looking at the things that are not seen. How can you look at things that are not seen? The answer is, of course, that we contact the eternal, not by our physical senses, but by faith. We contact the temporary by our senses; we contact the eternal by our faith.

A little farther on in the same epistle, Paul says that as Christians "we walk by faith, not by sight" (2 Corinthians 5:7 NKJV). In other words, we are not primarily influenced by the temporary things of this world that we contact with our senses. Instead, we walk by faith. We are directed, governed, controlled, and motivated by the things of the unseen world, which are eternal things.

In 2 Corinthians 3:18, Paul gives another extremely important and related revelation, that the eternal is revealed to us in the mirror of God's Word. In the New Testament, the Word of God is often compared to a mirror. We are told that this mirror does not show us our natural, physical body or outward appearance, but it shows us the unseen, eternal things— our spiritual nature and the things of the spiritual world.

> [18] *But we all, with unveiled face, beholding as in a mirror the glory of the Lord, are being transformed into the same image from glory to*

glory, just as by the Spirit of the Lord. (2 Corinthians 3:18 NKJV)

Again, the same principle is brought out. It is only while we look in the mirror of God's Word and see the eternal and the glory that God has prepared for us, that the Holy Spirit works on us to transform us into the likeness of that glory. If we take our eyes off the eternal, the Holy Spirit can no longer perform His transforming work in us. This is because Jesus is Lord of both the eternal and the temporal. He will bless us in both realms, but only if we keep our priorities right. If our priorities are wrong, then we miss the blessing of the Lord, and the Spirit of God is not able to work on us.

Moses is an example of a man who kept his priorities right. In Hebrews 11, we find this description of him:

²⁴ *By faith Moses, when he became of age, refused to be called the son of Pharaoh's daughter,*

²⁵ *choosing rather to suffer afflic-
tion with the people of God than to
enjoy the passing pleasures of sin,*

²⁶ *esteeming the reproach of Christ
greater riches than the treasures in
Egypt; for he looked to the reward.*

²⁷ *By faith he forsook Egypt, not
fearing the wrath of the king; for
he endured as seeing Him who is
invisible.*

(Hebrews 11:24–27 NKJV)

Notice the key clause, "he endured
as seeing Him who is invisible." That
is, he saw the eternal God, the eternal
realm, and the eternal realities. How
did Moses see them? Not with his
senses, but by faith. Because he con-
tacted the unseen eternal realities by
faith, he was not moved away from his
calling, and he did not lose his sense of
values. He did not regard the riches of
Egypt as greater than the eternal
riches of God. He was willing to forego
the riches of Egypt in order to attain to
the eternal riches of God. His priorities

were right, because by faith he kept his eyes on the unseen eternal realities.

In this connection, I want to give you a warning that is particularly important for people in our culture and civilization: Do not pursue riches. Do not make wealth your goal. Paul has something very sad and very solemn to say to Christians who pursue riches:

> [9] *People who want to get rich fall into temptation and a trap and into many foolish and harmful desires that plunge men into ruin and destruction.*

> [10] *For the love of money is a root of all kinds of evil. Some people, eager for money, have wandered from the faith and pierced themselves with many griefs.*

> [11] *But you, man of God, flee from all this, and pursue righteousness, godliness, faith, love, endurance and gentleness.*

> *(1 Timothy 6:9–11)*

Do not pursue riches. Pursue the eternal realities, the eternal riches. If you pursue the temporal riches, if you set your eyes on them and make them your goal, you are going to be sorry. You are going to pierce yourself through with many griefs. You are going to fall into a trap and into "many foolish and harmful desires that plunge men into ruin and destruction." Hear those words, and if your heart is set to pursue riches, turn back today.

I thank God that there is an alternative to pursuing riches. We can seek the kingdom of God and let God add to us what we need, in abundance, because God is not stingy, but generous. Once He sees that our motives are right, He can release His generosity toward us. Jesus says,

[31] *Therefore do not worry, saying, "What shall we eat?" or "What shall we drink?" or "What shall we wear?"*

³² *For after all these things the Gentiles seek. For your heavenly Father knows that you need all these things.*

³³ *But seek first the kingdom of God and His righteousness* [the eternal things], *and all these things* [the temporal things] *shall be added to you.*

(*Matthew 6:31–33* NKJV)

There is a great difference between pursuing the temporal, and pursuing the eternal and letting God add the temporal to you. You must have your priorities right.

CHAPTER TEN

Letting God Choose

My final bit of advice for those who want God's best is to let God choose for you.

I have been deeply impressed by a statement made by John the Baptist:

> [27] *John answered and said, "A man can receive nothing unless it has been given to him from heaven."* (John 3:27 NKJV)

John's disciples were reporting to him that the one whom he declared to be the Messiah was getting more disciples than he was, and they were expecting that somehow John would get upset about this. But he said, in effect, "So what? A man can receive nothing unless it has been given to him from heaven." Many preachers, churches, and religious groups often get upset if somebody else gets more church members, wins more converts, or has a larger ministry. But I think we need to cultivate that attitude of John, that a man can receive nothing unless it has been given to him from heaven.

At one time in my ministry, I realized I needed to learn that lesson very carefully. As I meditated on it, I said, "Lord, are you sure that's right? I see a lot of people getting things, and I don't see any evidence that they were given from heaven."

The Holy Spirit said to me, "There's a difference between grabbing and receiving." That opened my eyes! I saw so many people, Christians included, busy grabbing, out for all they could get. Many times they were ruthless and unethical in their dealings with fellow Christians and with their fellow human beings. They were just out for what they could get. And God said to me, "That's only grabbing. Whatever you get by grabbing, you will not have forever."

The only thing you will ultimately keep is what has been given to you from heaven. So, why go through all that labor and toil to grab and to get something that you will not be allowed to keep? Why not rest, turn your face toward God, and say, "God, show me what it is your good pleasure to give me"?

Jesus said to His disciples, "Do not fear, little flock, for it is your Father's good pleasure to give you the kingdom" (Luke 12:32 NKJV). Brothers and sisters, if we have the kingdom, why do we have to grab? We do not get the kingdom because we grab for it; we get the kingdom because it is God's good pleasure to give us the kingdom. We must learn to rest for a little while from grabbing and be willing to see what God wants to give. Many times when we grab and have that grabbing attitude, we are not in a condition to be able to receive what God is freely offering to us.

I spend much of the year in Israel, and there is a phrase that I hear so often: "I've got a right to this; it's mine!" That is a natural way to think, but it is not the way to think in the kingdom of God. In the kingdom of God, we say, "God, my Father, what is it your good pleasure to give me?" That is the only thing that matters. That is the only thing that is permanent.

God said to His people, Israel, in Psalm 47:

[2] *For the LORD Most High is to be feared, A great King over all the earth.*

³*He subdues peoples under us,*
And nations under our feet.

⁴*He chooses our inheritance for us,*
The glory of Jacob whom He loves.
(Psalm 47:2–4 NASB)

God did not tell Israel to go out and look for the best piece of land and grab it. He said He would give them a place that He had chosen. In connection with that land, He uses the word *glory*. The Bible says elsewhere that Israel's land is the glory of all lands, the beautiful land, the desirable land. God chose much better for them than they would ever have chosen for themselves. When it was a question of their getting their inheritance, He fought for them, and He subdued nations under their feet.

If we go out and grab, we do not have God fighting for us. And if we go out and grab, we will probably get in a war that we are going to lose. There is no need to grab, for God will do everything that is needed to bring us into our inheritance.

Another vital point from the Bible is that our inheritance is the only place we can know true rest. Moses said to Israel, when they were still east of the Jordan, "For as yet you have not come to the rest and the inheritance which the LORD your God is giving you" (Deuteronomy 12:9 NKJV).

Notice that God was giving them their inheritance, and when they came into their inheritance, then they would come into their rest. Why are there so many restless Christians in the world? Because they have never come into their inheritance. Why have they never come into their inheritance? Because they have never allowed God to give it to them. Why have they never allowed God to give it to them? Because they have thought they had to grab it for themselves.

I have a few more important points to make concerning what God gives us. First, there is a tremendous statement made by Jesus in John

10:29 (NRSV): "What my Father has given me is greater than all." This is the marginal version in more than one of the modern translations. I have looked at the original Greek text and believe this is the best authenticated original text.

"What my Father has given me is greater than all." That is a breathtaking statement! Ultimately, the most important and irresistible thing in the universe, the one thing that is absolutely sure, settled, and cannot be challenged or overthrown, is the thing that the Father has given. That is greater than all. It is something that no power of hell or demons or evil rulers can ever undo, overthrow, or unsettle.

It was characteristic of Jesus that He never wanted anything except what the Father had given. There was no force that could ever take from Jesus what the Father had given. What is true of Him is true, in like measure, of you and me. What the Father has given to you and me is greater than all. Do not get nervous or uptight about the opposition. The very fact that you get uptight is evidence that you are really not moving into what the Father has given you. If you know the Father has given it to you, you can smile at the opposition. It is absolutely guaranteed. The supreme factor in the course of the universe is what God the Father has given.

These are the words of Jesus from the Sermon on the Mount: "Blessed are the meek, for they will inherit the earth." (Matthew 5:5). Can you understand that? They do not have to grab the earth; they are going to inherit it. The grabbers will be done away with. There will be an end to all the grabbers—the greedy, the unscrupulous, the covetous, the violent, and the wicked. The Bible says they will be no more. You will search for the wicked man, and you will not even find his place. However, the meek will inherit the earth. It is so important to learn to let God choose our inheritance for us and to understand that what the Father has given is greater than all.

Let me close this book on receiving God's best with a quotation that I once heard: "God gives His best to those who leave the choice to Him." Are you willing to leave the choice to your Father?

To summarize, I will list the things you must do if you want God's best:

1. Want God's best. Do not settle for less.

2. Focus on Jesus.

3. Meditate on God's Word.

4. Make friends with the Holy Spirit.

5. Hear and promptly obey God's voice.

6. Be careful how and what you hear.

7. Be more concerned with the eternal than the temporary. Make sure your priorities are right.

8. Let God choose for you.

About the Author

Derek Prince was born in India of British parents. He was educated as a scholar of Greek and Latin at two of Britain's most famous educational institutions: Eton College and Cambridge University. From 1940 to 1949, he held a Fellowship (equivalent to a resident professorship) in Ancient and Modern Philosophy at King's College, Cambridge. He also studied Hebrew and Aramaic, both at Cambridge University and at the Hebrew University in Jerusalem. In addition, he speaks a number of modern languages.

In the early years of World War II, while serving as a hospital attendant with the British Army, Derek Prince experienced a life-changing encounter with Jesus Christ, concerning which he writes,

> Out of this encounter, I formed two conclusions which I have never since had reason to change: first, that Jesus Christ is alive; second, that the Bible is a true, relevant, up-to-date book. These two conclusions radically and permanently altered the whole course of my life.

Derek Prince's nondenominational, nonsectarian approach has opened doors for his teaching to people from many different racial and religious backgrounds, and he is internationally recognized as one of the leading Bible expositors of our time. His daily radio broadcast, *Today with Derek Prince*, reaches more than half the globe, as it is translated into Arabic, five Chinese languages (Mandarin, Amoy, Cantonese, Shanghaiese, Swatow), Mongolian, Spanish, Russian, and Tongan. He has published more than thirty books, which have been translated into more than fifty foreign languages.

Through the Global Outreach Leaders Program of Derek Prince Ministries, his books and audio cassettes are sent free of charge to hundreds of national Christian leaders in the Third World, Eastern Europe, and Russia.

Now past the age of seventy-five, Derek Prince still travels the world—imparting God's revealed truth, praying for the sick and afflicted, and sharing his prophetic insight into world events in the light of Scripture.

The international base of Derek Prince Ministries is located in Charlotte, North Carolina, with branch offices in Australia, Canada, Germany, Holland, New Zealand, South Africa, and the United Kingdom.